SINGLE AND THE RIGHT WAY TO MINGLE

Dr. Ron Webb

Copyright © 2018 by **Dr. Ron Webb**

All rights reserved. No part of this book may be used or reproduced by any means, graphic, electronic, or mechanical, including photocopying, recording, taping or by any information storage retrieval system without the written permission of the publisher except in the case of brief quotations embodied in critical articles and reviews.

Dr. Ron Webb/Rejoice Essential Publishing

PO BOX 512
Effingham, SC 29541

www.republishing.org

Author's website: www.ronwebbministries.com

Photography by Corey Matthews

Copyright © 2018 Dr. Ron Webb

Unless otherwise indicated, Scripture is taken from the King James Version.

All rights reserved.

Single And The Right Way To Mingle/ Dr. Ron Webb
ISBN-10: 1-946756-28-8
ISBN-13: 978-1-946756-28-2
Library of Congress Control Number: 2018940618

TABLE OF CONTENTS

FOREWORD..1

INTRODUCTION..6

CHAPTER 1:   Happily Single................8

CHAPTER 2:   Soaking Season...............13

CHAPTER 3:   The Danger of Rebound Romance..........16

CHAPTER 4:   The Pain of Breaking Up.....................20

CHAPTER 5:   Investigate Before You Participate............24

CHAPTER 6:   Lured by Loneliness.....................34

CHAPTER 7:   The Bait You Use Determines the Fish You Catch.....................37

CHAPTER 8:   Private Property..............40

CHAPTER 9:   Destiny Dating vs. Shotgun Dating............44

CHAPTER 10:	Looking For Love In All the Wrong Places..............................47
CHAPTER 11:	Don't Preheat the Oven If Your Not Cooking Anything...........52
CHAPTER 12:	Unrealistic Expectations....................58
CHAPTER 13:	Avoid Abusive Relationships...................61
CHAPTER 14:	Live-Ins Are Fill-Ins...............................66
CHAPTER 15:	Believers Don't Marry Unbelievers..........70
CHAPTER 16:	Lying Lovers...................75
CHAPTER 17:	Burden of Baggage.........79
CHAPTER 18:	Staying Faithful In the Field..........................84
CHAPTER 19:	Committed Relationships.....................89
CHAPTER 20:	The Importance of Communication...............94

CHAPTER 21:   Put a Ring on It................99

REFERENCES...104

ABOUT THE AUTHOR............................107

FOREWORD

Dating can be stressful. Many people have a fear of starting all over again to meet someone new. Some have been hurt previously by a failed relationship and hesitate to take another shot at love. Others may feel like they're too old, and some think it's a hopeless case for them. These were all the reasons why I didn't date anyone for many years. *Single and The Right Way to Mingle*, by Dr. Ron Webb, is a lifeline when it comes to dating. I wish it was written when I was feeling depressed and lonely in my singleness.

This book covers various aspects of the dating process and beyond that many people must know. For instance, Dr. Webb discusses how the bait we use determines the fish we catch. I wished someone told me what I needed to know those years when I was attracting all the wrong men before I gave my life to the Lord. He also discusses the importance of the preparation stage.

I realized the significance of preparing for marriage when I went through a bad breakup. I thought my life was over, and I didn't know how to go on with life. I cried out to God, and He took me through the necessary process of healing. Once my heart was healed, I applied the principles that Dr. Webb teaches, and I was ready to mingle again.

I was no longer looking for love in all the wrong places. I set guidelines for my next relationship. I even set standards and never compromised. I looked beyond my current situation and prepared for my future by getting an education and starting a business. I knew I had something to bring to the relationship. Dr. Webb emphasizes having realistic expectations.

When I had reasonable expectations that were obtainable, the right man was able to find me when I was staying faithful in my field, which is another area Dr. Webb covers in *Single and The Right Way to Mingle*. My husband, Tron, was everything I could ever want in a man.

When I read the pages in *Single and The Right Way to Mingle*, I was encouraged. This book surpasses any superficial dating material and gets to the core issues to strengthen any relationship such as finances, family, religion, commitment, boundaries, and more. I applied what I read and discussed it with my spouse. We both were blessed by the material. This book proved to be an effective communication tool since it asks many questions that must be talked about in relationships.

My favorite parts of this book are the application questions at the end of each chapter. I'm able to apply what I learned and reflect on the material I just read. This book is a must-read for singles as well as those who are in a committed relationship.

Kimberly Moses, CEO
Rejoice Essential Magazine

***

Being Single and a Christian Man or Woman has its perks, but at the same time, there are many unknowns when it comes to finding the one who will say, "I do" and be completely right for you. It's nice to have a guideline to follow while single and on the prowl! This is the perfect book that gives you the feedback you need to stay ahead of the game. It's what you have been looking for but no one has put out there! I'm definitely going to use this as a Q&A when choosing my significant other. This is the Final Stop before you close up the Shop! Suit up Singles; it's time to Mingle!

Evangelist Amber Brown

Author of Rise To The Mission

***

It's not a curse, a disorder, a deficiency, or even a flaw that you're SINGLE. You can embrace it and realize you have an amazing opportunity to be in a relationship with the most important person you will ever know—YOU! No one can date you, court you, make you laugh, and know what makes you tick more than you and God. In the pages of this book, Dr. Ron Webb gives singles a fresh perspective on taking advantage of this special time, YOUR discovery time, by giving you the tools to learn how your uniqueness is specifically designed for the one God is preparing for you. So, in the meantime, take yourself out on dates, go on a vacation with yourself, spend time with your cat, dog, or fish. Most importantly, get in touch with the Word of God, it's your roadmap for knowing all about yourself.

Kathy (Kat) Sneed On-Air Personality, Music Director, and Host of "Sounds of the Heartland" at KLUH Life Radio 90.3 FM

***

Dr. Ron Webb is not afraid to address the issues that are so often overlooked in Christian dating. In this book no topic is left unaddressed or confronted. One of my favorite chapters is "Soaking Season" which discusses the importance of preparing yourself for the mate God has for you. *Single and The Right Way to Mingle* is definitely a must read for anyone seeking a godly mate, God's way!

Jacqueline Henry

***

Being single doesn't mean being alone or lonely, but it's discovering who you are. When you know you're worth and value and that you're healthy and whole, you won't settle for a Bozo but you will wait on your Boaz. Know the difference in a good man and a God man. In this book, it will challenge you that although you may feel lonely but you are never alone.

Emma Gilmer

***

In Dr. Ron Webb's book, "Single And The Right Way to Mingle" he deals with the severity and realness of potential relationships, and how it is vital to not jump into a new relationship just to feel validated and loved. He breaks down and redefines the "Rebound Relationship" from a Godly perspective, in a way that anyone who has ever experienced a breakup could understand. Dr. Webb talks about the importance of waiting, healing, and not settling. For anyone who has or who may be still experiencing the hurt of a breakup, this is a must-read.

Lauren Cassinger

***

This book on dating is needed in the church today, due to the fact that there isn't a lot of teaching on the topic. To be saved and single is one thing, but you need a scriptural strategy to be effective in it. The chapter on "Destiny Dating" is powerful. We should prioritize our purpose over our preference. Dr. Ron Webb, the author presents to us a great tool for all singles to use.

Kendall Morris

***

This book is a must-read for single Christian men and women, as we are all looking for that match made in heaven as always Dr. Ron Webb speaks to the crux of the matter, he has specific instructions about how detrimental it is to bring the baggage from past relationships into your future. As all his books are, this is based on scriptures from the word of God! Again, a must read!

Lawrence Freeman

***

INTRODUCTION

During the years I've been in ministry, I've counseled many couples. I've also witnessed divorce happening at an alarming rate due to people making bad choices. Perhaps these choices could've been avoided if they would've sought marriage counseling before they said "I do". Marriage counseling is important because it helps bring out so much that wasn't noticed just by Q&A. I'm passionate about seeing people have blessed and prosperous marriages. This is why I'm focusing on the single ministry to cut down on the divorce rate in my community. There are certain things that need to be addressed before a person says, "I do" and walks down the aisle.

A lot of singles ask me about courtship; I share with them certain principles that I applied when I was courting my wife. These guidelines are the foundation that every single must know in order to have a successful relationship. This book will also give key steps to lead you in the right direction while dating.

I believe in doing things God's way, and there are biblical-based principles to help you. They will encourage you to seek Him before making your decisions. So many are deceived and blinded when it comes to dating or relationships, but you're too cute to be cursed and too fine to fail! Wait on God to send you the right one. You are not a lottery!

CHAPTER 1

HAPPILY SINGLE

Can you really be happily single? Yes, you can! Many people feel like being single is a bad thing. That's not true. You can be content while being single. The Apostle Paul was happily single, but he encouraged others to marry if they wanted to. He knew that he could do more for the Lord being single. He had the gift of celibacy (1 Corinthians 7:7) or made a choice to be single and not marry. 1 Corinthians 7:32-35 explains how married men and women are more concerned with the world, such as pleasing their spouse, and their interests are divided between them and the Lord. He further explains that an unmarried person is concerned about the Lord's affairs and how they can please Him.

Let's explore four statements that will prove that you can be happily single.

1. Single is not a status.

It's a word that describes a person who's strong enough to live and enjoy life without depending on others. You may be used to having someone around at all times or always sharing things with others, but in reality, is if you can't enjoy yourself or enjoy being single, then its very unlikely for someone to fill that void.

Being single gives you time to be by yourself and with yourself, and in doing so you get to discover yourself. Finally, a time to reconnect with yourself, talk to yourself (yes, I said talk to yourself), and discover your purpose in life and begin to walk in it.

Many people get lost while in a relationship, but never fulfill their destiny. The right person will be in alignment with your destiny. When you're single, you have time to prepare for marriage. You can work on your credit, character flaws, and getting established in your career. This is a time of reflection and a time of acceptance and letting go.

2. If you don't let go of the past, you can never appreciate the future!

It's okay to have fine memories of your past, but remember, that was the past. So, don't curse it, don't nurse it, and don't rehearse it. You must stop clinging to them and embrace today. Remember yesterday is in the tomb of time and tomorrow is in the womb of time. Yesterday is history and tomorrow is a mystery. Stop holding on to a painful past. Press out to a bright and fabulous future.

Philippians 3:13 says, "Brethren, I count not myself to have apprehended: but this one thing I do, forgetting those things which are behind, and reaching forth unto those things which are before." Apostle Paul even wrote that he would keep on pressing toward the future. Your future is bright in God.

Isaiah 43:18-19 says, "Remember ye not the former things, neither consider the things of old. Behold, I will do a new thing; now it shall spring forth; shall ye not know it? I will even make a way in the wilderness, and rivers in the desert." The Bible warns us not to dwell on the past because God wants to do new things in our lives. He can make a way for us when we go through trying times.

3. Sometimes it's only when you've lost some things that you're free to find out what you were missing.

You've been putting all your energy into relationships, but instead, how about focusing on yourself. Complete yourself, date yourself, encourage yourself, and enjoy yourself.

Change can be healthy, and it can bring healing. Imagine the idea of meeting new people, new environments, new adventures, traveling, and more. Don't be afraid to start over again. Don't be afraid to love again. Okay, you went through a messy break up; your heart has been bruised, battered, tattered, torn, and broken, but you're going to love again and trust again. The next person will treat you right and treasure you. As long as you've heeded the steps and warnings in this book, they'll respect you, honor you, and esteem you.

4. Being single is not the end of the world.

There are other problems more depressing than worrying about singleness. Be thankful that you're living and still have friends and family. The world has not ended. Yes, I know all your friends are married or are in relationships but be thankful! Hold your head up and put a smile on your face.

It's been said that in order to see a rainbow, you have to go through the storm. When something bad happens, we tend to focus on the negatives and forget there must be something positive hidden in the havoc. We all know these words are a lot easier to say than to practice, but if we look to God for guidance, he'll strengthen us in our struggles.

APPLICATION QUESTIONS

1. Describe the term single.

   _____
   _____
   _____
   _____
   _____

2. What are the benefits of being happily single?

   _____
   _____
   _____
   _____
   _____

3. What was Apostle Paul's view point on being single compared to marriage?

_____
_____
_____
_____
_____

4. Why is it important to know yourself before dating?

_____
_____
_____
_____
_____

CHAPTER 2

SOAKING SEASON

What exactly is a soaking season? Well, it's more like a waiting season; waiting for the right time and the right moment. Your personal soaking season is your time of preparation designed to get you ready for your blessing. To gain a greater understanding of soaking season, let's look at the inspiring story of Queen Esther in the Bible. Esther's story shows us the importance of waiting on the Lord.

In Esther chapter two, when King Xerxes (Ahasuerus) was replacing Queen Vashti because she refused to come at his command; many fair maidens were being purified in the women's chamber (v. 2). These maidens received a year's worth of beauty treatments consisting olive oil, myrrh, perfumes, and cosmetics in preparation to meet the King and perhaps chosen to be his Queen. Esther soaked for one whole year for one night with the King.

Esther 2:12 says, "Now when every maid's turn was come to go in to king Ahasuerus, after that she had been twelve months, according to the manner of the women, (for so were the days of their purifications accomplished, to wit, six months with oil of myrrh, and six months with sweet odours, and with other things for the purifying of the women.)"

By the way, men have soaking seasons too. This is the time where men should be preparing for their future wife. Every man needs to be gainfully employed; every man needs to provide a place of shelter for your wife to be. No woman wants to live with in-laws, with no privacy. It's like being married and bound. Although, she may not comment for a while, in her heart, she wants her own home, her own bathroom, her own kitchen, etc. Every woman wants and needs a good provider and protector, so before you say "I do" to marriage, make sure you say "I do" to your soaking season.

If you rush through your soaking season, you'll bankrupt your chance of success by taking a whole lot more than you're giving in the relationship. For instance, when it comes to finances. One person may feel like they're carrying most of the burden in a relationship if they're the only one working while the other person spends money carelessly.

Likewise, when only one person is emotionally involved, and the other person isn't, the person bearing the emotional load will be hurt because the partner isn't investing the same amount of emotional support into the relationship.

Your soaking season will make sure you pass the love test because you took the time to prepare. The next time when someone asks what you do in your spare time say, "I'm just soaking." When someone asks why you're not dating just respond with, "Oh, I'm just soaking."

APPLICATION QUESTIONS

1. What is a soaking season?

   _____
   _____
   _____
   _____

2. What is the importance of a soaking season?

   _____
   _____
   _____
   _____

3. In what ways do men have soaking seasons?

   _____
   _____
   _____
   _____

4. How are you preparing for your next relationship in your soaking season?

   _____
   _____
   _____
   _____

CHAPTER 3

THE DANGER OF REBOUND ROMANCE

It is so important while preparing to date to make sure you're healed from a previous relationship. I've witnessed firsthand the pain of past relationships spilling over into a new relationship, only to watch it become a recipe for disaster. Why is it so important to wait and get totally healed? Because when you're rebounding, you tend to try to replace a love that you lost or perhaps try to forget a relationship you were in. Neither one is good for you. They both will affect you, whether you dumped them, or they dumped you; it really doesn't matter.

You'll start out with a lot of baggage and unrealistic expectations, so please allow yourself time to heal. Now, on the flip side, if you both realize that this is a rebound relationship, and you're not intending to be in it a long time, you need to have that understanding at the beginning. If not, then you're setting yourself up for failure. Beware of people who will prey on your vulnerability. You may have just come out of a relationship, and you probably miss the other person like crazy. You might even be super emotional. People can sense this and will take advantage of it. The next thing you know, you're in another relationship. This is a huge mistake.

If you don't allow yourself to heal, you'll spend the rest of your life in revenge mode. When you rebound, you'll end up letting it spill over into a fresh relationship. When your new boyfriend or girlfriend gets tired of hearing it over and over again, they are ready to bounce too. Your new boyfriend or girlfriend doesn't want to hear about your ex all the time. If you continue to bring up your ex, you're not over that person, and that soul tie needs to be broken. In the end, you end up hurting your new boyfriend or girlfriend because they know deep down that you aren't over your ex.

Psalm 34:18-19 says, "The Lord is nigh unto them that are of a broken heart; and saveth such as be of a contrite spirit. Many are the afflictions of the righteous: but the Lord delivereth him out of them all."

When you rebound, you hurt yourself by not allowing yourself to heal. Shut the door to your heart to people for a little while and allow God to heal it. People who are rebounding may be covering emotions they don't want to deal with such as depression, loneliness, low self-esteem, rejection, and anxiety. God knows how to deliver you if you cry out for His help. God wants to bring healing to your heart. Will you allow Him to take you through the necessary process?

Rebound dating doesn't have the same feeling as you'd have in a committed relationship. If you're constantly bashing your ex, that's another sign that you're still dealing with a lot of raw feelings. It's because you want them to feel what you're feeling, so when you carry that bitterness into another relationship, it's highly likely to fail and end on very bad terms.

So, if you're going to rebound, make it count for something. Don't repeat the process. Remember, Henry Ford said, "You always get what you always got if you always do what you've always done." Don't jump into another relationship while trying to run from your true feelings. No matter how much you think you'll fall or how bad the pain is, God will pick you back up again. Deuteronomy 33:27 says, "The eternal God is thy refuge, and underneath are the everlasting arms."

APPLICATION QUESTIONS

1. What are some dangers of rebound romance?

   _____
   _____
   _____
   _____
   _____

2. Why do some people rebound?

   _____
   _____
   _____
   _____
   _____

3. Why is it important to allow God to heal you before entering into another relationship?

_____
_____
_____
_____
_____

4. Is there any success when it comes to rebound relationships?

_____
_____
_____
_____
_____

CHAPTER 4

THE PAIN OF BREAKING UP

Severing ties from a past relationship can be painful and traumatic all at the same time. Creating a bond is easy but letting go can be very difficult. Separation of any kind can crush your spirit whether it's from a job, marriage, loved one, or friendship. One of the hardest things in breaking up is trying to readjust your life without that person. When ending a relationship, be prepared to experience some withdraw symptoms of emotions. Some examples of withdraw symptoms can be longing to see that person, longing to hear their voice, or even longing to reconnect the relationship. If you are not careful these withdraw symptoms can steer you in the wrong direction tempting you to reconnect to what God has told you to separate from.

    The recovery of a breakup can be a slow and painful process, but don't be discouraged because with the help of the Lord you can get through it! Psalms 147:3 says, "He heals the brokenhearted and binds up their wounds." Be encouraged knowing that God is going to heal your broken heart. He is going to heal the very area that is causing you great pain.

Don't allow the pain of a breakup to get you off course or cause you to blame others for your pain. Stop reliving the pain in your mind and start thinking on what God has ahead for you. Just accept this breakup as a lesson learned and use it as a tool of preparation for your next relationship.

If you are experiencing the pain of a break up here are a few tips on how to deal with the pain:

1. Make the decision to let go.

First know, that it takes effort to let something go. Refusing to let go can sabotage any efforts you have to moving forward. It is also important to stop reliving every detail of the breakup in your mind. You can't move forward if you are too busy living backwards.

2. Express your pain and responsibility.

Express the pain, the hurt, and how you felt. Get it out in the open and out of your system. Vent to a friend, pray about it, but keep it moving! Don't play the victim role. Even if it makes you feel good playing the victim role, don't succumb to it! Yes, you were hurt and heartbroken, but you must move on. Don't allow this pain to become your identity. Take responsibility by learning from this experience and use this situation as a life lesson to improve your next relationship. It is up to you to use this experience as a learning tool.

3. Focus on the present.

When you focus on the present, you have less time to dwell on the past. When the feelings of the past creep into your mind, you must immediately reject them and focus on the new. Remember, if you only crowd your thoughts with experiences from the past you eliminate room for the present. Recognize that focusing on the past is only a distraction and it will drain you of your joy. Focusing on your present will allow you to live your life to the fullest.

4. Forgive them and then forgive yourself.

Forgiveness isn't saying, "I agree with what you did," but instead, "I don't agree with what you did, but I choose to forgive you, anyway." You must forgive to move forward. Forgiveness is not a sign of weakness but instead it's saying, "I'm a good person and you're a good person but even though you did something that hurt me, I want to move forward with my life and welcome joy back into it. And I can't fully do that until I forgive you and let you go." By doing this it turns your breakup into a breakthrough! Remember, forgiveness is for you and it will help you on your road to recovery.

APPLICATION QUESTIONS

1. What positive strategies can you use to move forward from a past relationship?

   _____
   _____
   _____
   _____

2. How can expressing your feelings be beneficial after a painful breakup?

_____
_____
_____
_____

3. Why is forgiveness a powerful tool in moving forward?

_____
_____
_____
_____

4. How can dwelling on your past be detrimental to your future?

_____
_____
_____
_____

CHAPTER 5

INVESTIGATE BEFORE YOU PARTICIPATE

In the business world, no company or organization will hire you without a resume or an interview and in most cases, a background check. If you don't meet their specific requirements, you don't get the job. Relationships should be handled the same way. Today's generation moves first, then asks questions later. This is all wrong. You need to ask questions first, then pursue later. Why is that so important? It is important because the world we live in is full of deception. People lie; they only give you the pretty-sounding story and leave out the ugly parts. But the part left out tends to be the most destructive.

What are some of the right questions to ask?

1. Are you saved, single, and satisfied with yourself? Because if you're not happy with you, no one else can totally fulfill you. Sorry, but it's true.
2. What are your family values? We believe in honoring and respecting our parents as stated in the fourth commandment. We believe in Christian character as

taught in the Bible and in unity and working together. We believe that a man should be gainfully employed with a good job.

Investigation (Looking for Love)

You want a Holy Ghost hook up, not a hook up from Hell.
Hell date equals stalemate.
You may be fly, but not be my guy.
No contract; no contact.
No wed; no bed.
No ringy; no dingy.
Investigate before you participate.

Trust me, it's better to deal with the hurt right up front than to build a relationship only to discover later that you've embraced a lie or didn't know the whole story.

Through careful study and prayer, ask God to show you what you need to know and what you should do before you become too attached. Remember, the heart isn't a toy thing; it's a joy thing. If you put your heart out there to be played with, it's hard to reel it back in.

Don't Ignore the Signs

One of the worst things you can do after completing your investigation is to act as if the results you see don't exist. As the old saying goes, "It is what it is." If the light is red, don't run the red light. Stop! If the light is yellow, don't speed up and try to beat the light; slow down and wait. If the light is green, proceed with caution, but don't act like you don't see what you see.

1. If he/she has a bad temper and constantly flies off the handle, put a check by it.
2. If he/she acts overly jealous and has a serious insecurity problem, put a check by it.
3. If they disrespect you openly in the presence of others, put a check by it.
4. If they embarrass you publicly or privately, put a check by it.
5. If you have children and they mistreat, dishonor, or disrespect your children, put two checks by it.
6. If they are selfish, self-serving, and all about themselves, put a check by it.

This is only the short list. Don't fool yourself into thinking you can change that person. If they're not willing to make some changes or alter some things, then that may be your sign to keep moving on.

On the other hand, if the signs are good, continue to move slowly if he/she values and respects you and his/her self. An unselfish person who puts the needs of others above their own is a good sign that you're on the right track. I promise, you'll never be sorry for investigating.

When you buy a new car, you just don't drive it off the lot without carefully inspecting or test-driving it. If you buy a piece of real estate, you order a title search. It's wise to treat dating the same way. It'll save you lots of headaches and lots of heartaches, God knows.

Investigate! Investigate! Investigate!

We discussed how many people rush into a relationship without thoroughly investigating or doing their research on the person they're dating. There must be a standard when it comes to Christian dating. Don't waiver. Don't compromise. No means no. We should be God pleasers, not people pleasers. We should be spirit led. Set the standard and then stick to it. In other words, remain faithful to your values and enjoy the benefits. Proverbs 28:20 says, "A faithful man shall abound with blessings." As you remain faithful, you'll be dating in God's way.

Stick to the Standard

1. I will put my future in God's hands.
2. I will learn to be content as a single person.
3. I will save sex for marriage.
4. I will learn to say no.
5. I will seek God's will for my life.
6. I will guard my heart.
7. I will date only Christians.
8. I will seriously consider courtship.

To bring a greater level of understanding, let's take a closer look at these guidelines.

The first guideline is putting our future in God's hands. Some people have a hard time letting go and letting God take control. They map out their whole life while never realizing that God can interrupt our plans to do what's necessary in our lives. We need to realize that God's plans for our lives are better than ours.

Jeremiah 29:11 says, "For I know the thoughts that I think toward you, saith the Lord, thoughts of peace, and not of evil, to give you an expected end."

It's all about yielding to Him. It means letting our agenda be replaced with His. We'll desire everything God wants for us in a potential spouse. We'll look for someone who'll be in alignment with our destiny in the Kingdom of God. We'll wait for God's timing to meet the right person and pursue the ultimate goal of marriage.

The second guideline is learning how to be content as a single person. The Apostle Paul wrote that he learned to be content in whatever state he was in because he wanted nothing more than the fellowship with Jesus.

Philippians 4:11 says, "Not that I speak in respect of want: for I have learned, in whatsoever state I am, therewith to be content."

Paul's relationship with Jesus was priority one, and it should be the same with us. Jesus should be number one, and anything else that is in the number one slot is considered an idol. God hates idols (Deuteronomy 16:21-22) and will attack anything in your life He sees as such. When you're content as a single person, you have the opportunity to know yourself which will keep you from getting lost in a bad relationship. You also won't be anxious about getting married. God tells us not to be anxious about anything.

Philippians 4:6 (ESV) says, "Do not be anxious about anything, but in everything by prayer and supplication with thanksgiving let your requests be made known to God."

The third guideline is saving sex for marriage. Sexual intercourse between a man and a woman outside of marriage is called fornication.[1] God hates sin but has a special hatred for fornication. The Bible says to flee fornication (run from it, not run to it).

That's what Joseph did. He lost his coat, but kept his character. (Genesis 39:7-12). Why does the Bible say flee? Because no one can stand up to it. Your sex drive will drive you crazy! 1 Thessalonians 4:3 says, "This is the will of God that you abstain from fornication." Don't let fornication become your vocation. This sin destroys the beautiful plan that God has in his mind for you. If you're a Christian, your body is the temple of the Holy Ghost. 1 Thessalonians 4:4,6 says, "Everyone should know how to possess his body in sanctification (purity) and honor, that no man go beyond and defraud his brother in any matter."

Defrauding is raising expectations in another person which you cannot rightfully fulfill. In business, defrauding is cheating or leading someone to expect certain benefits which you know are false. When a guy professes to love a girl and talks about getting married someday in order to entice her to have sex with him, that is defrauding.

On the flip side of that coin, a woman who expects a man to marry her because they're having sex or living together is deceiving herself. She's lying to herself, believing that he loves her. If he truly loved her, he'd want what was best for her. Yet, I've seen couples whereafter as many as five years, the guy simply walks away, and the woman is devastated because she had fooled herself into believing they had true love.

The fourth guideline is learning when to say no. You don't have to say yes to something when you should say no, especially if it's going to affect your relationship with Jesus Christ. You are valued in the eyes of God. You are a royal priesthood.

1 Peter 2:9 says, "But ye are a chosen generation, a royal priesthood, an holy nation, a peculiar people; that ye should

shew forth the praises of him who hath called you out of darkness into his marvelous light."

You are God's elect (Romans 8:33). There must be a standard. You are worth the catch. There must be boundaries established early in the relationship. Say no to shacking up. Say no to premarital sex. Say no to ungodly conversations. Say no to touching private areas. Say no to anything and everything that opens the door for the enemy to come in.

The fifth guideline is wanting God's will for your life. Many people die, sometimes prematurely, filled with books, ideas, and businesses because God's will wasn't fulfilled in their lives. People get so busy that they rush their time in prayer and never seek the Lord on what He wants before they act. They only seek Him when things fall apart.

Proverbs 19:21 says, "There are many devices in a man's heart; nevertheless, the counsel of the Lord, that shall stand."

God's way or no way means God's will instead of your will. Seek the will of God for a spouse. God will warn you about a person if they aren't right for you. You're God's child and He wants the best for you.

The sixth guideline is guarding your heart. The Bible tells us to guard our hearts because the issues of life flows from it (Proverbs 4:23). This is all about having wisdom. God will give us a generous portion of wisdom if we ask (James 1:5). To add the icing on the cake, God will give us sound wisdom if we walk uprightly (Proverbs 2:7).

Do you really want to get emotionally involved with someone who isn't equally invested? Do you really want to pour out your heart to someone who you don't really know? Do you really want to allow someone you don't fully trust to walk all over your heart? These are some of the questions we must ask ourselves.

The seventh guideline is dating only Christians. Many people feel like they can change another person. They make the mistake of believing that their looks or actions can convict someone to do what they want them to do. You can't change the heart of another; only God can do that. Don't be unequally yoked!

2 Corinthians 6:14 says, "Be ye not unequally yoked together with unbelievers: for what fellowship hath righteousness with unrighteousness? And what communion hath light with darkness?"

A yoke can be considered a partnership, teaming up with or bound together. There are two different value systems at work when a Christian dates a non-Christian. How will this relationship work out in the end, especially if the Christian is called into ministry full-time? How can they work with a spouse who doesn't understand the demands of ministry and who's spiritually immature to handle to attacks of the enemy?

The eighth guideline is to seriously consider courtship. Courtship is the activities that occur when people are developing a romantic relationship that could lead to marriage or the period of time when such activities occur.[2] The end result of courtship is marriage. Why waste your time on someone who isn't serious about you? If they won't commit to you, perhaps they're seeing other people on the side and having fun dating.

Some people get tired of waiting because they're getting older and truly want to settle down. They don't have time to play games. When you consider courtship, you become serious about who you choose to spend your time with. You're truly looking for great characteristics that you want in a potential spouse. Time is valuable, and it's something you can't get back.

APPLICATION QUESTIONS

1. Why should people investigate before they participate in dating?

   _____
   _____
   _____
   _____
   _____

2. What are some of the negative signs that we should not overlook when it comes to dating?

   _____
   _____
   _____
   _____
   _____

3. Why is it important to stick to standards in dating? What are some standards in dating?

   _____
   _____
   _____
   _____
   _____

4. Explain the term defrauding. Has it ever happened to you?

_____
_____
_____
_____
_____

CHAPTER 6

LURED BY LONELINESS

The spirit of loneliness has hit many people and has caused discouragement, which leads to depression. Be careful not to be sucked in by loneliness. Social isolation kills people more than obesity does. So many people are slowly dying inside. No connection with the reality of rejection. Al Green sang a song, "I'm so tired of being alone, I'm so tired of on my own..." You can be around a lot of people or even in a room full of people, and you can still be lonely. The movies, bookstores, parks, museums, beaches, and ball games are examples of places full of people where you can still feel all alone.

The spirit of loneliness is breaking many hearts today. Many will not fess up and admit how lonely and desperate they are. It seems as if there's a prescription for everything but loneliness. Men get lonely. Women get lonely. Rich people get lonely, and the poor get lonely. There's an epidemic of loneliness in today's disconnected world. Many fear dying alone.

So, what's the danger in loneliness? Opening your heart to anyone and everyone, which is a major setup for failure. Now, the devil is tricky. He pursues those who are lonely and vulnerable. I've seen people do very unwise things because they were lonely. They give out their phone number and put all their personal information out there on social media, and now they've become easy prey for the enemy. That's when they end up settling because they simply don't want to be alone.

1 Peter 5:8 says, "Be sober, be vigilant; because your adversary the devil, as a roaring lion, walketh about, seeking whom he may devour."

I spoke to an individual who said they started a relationship, not really interested in the person but just wanting to be with someone. They ended up having sex, although they didn't enjoy it, but were willing to sacrifice their values simply because of loneliness. God said that it's not good for man to be alone (Genesis 2:18). So, I want to encourage you by telling you to HOLD ON!

APPLICATION QUESTIONS

1. How are people lured by loneliness?

_____
_____
_____
_____
_____

2. What is the danger in loneliness?

_____
_____
_____
_____
_____

3. What ways can you ensure that you won't be lured by loneliness?

   _____
   _____
   _____
   _____
   _____

4. What advice would you give a single person who is depressed because they are lonely?

   _____
   _____
   _____
   _____
   _____

CHAPTER 7

THE BAIT YOU USE DETERMINES THE FISH YOU CATCH

Two of my favorite hobbies happen to be fishing and hunting, but I'll focus on fishing for now. Whenever someone goes fishing, they must bait their hook with something that attracts the fish. To bait means to entice or lure an animal with food.[3] Bait comes in many varieties: shape, color, texture, etc. Different species of fish will be more attracted to certain types of bait, and certain baits will be more effective in certain bodies of water, such as lakes, ponds, oceans, gulfs, rivers, or seas. It takes a great level of skill, research, or trial and error to master fishing. The same concept can be applied to dating.

There's nothing worse than trying to fish with bait that doesn't look the part. The fish you want to catch might not be in the pond you're fishing in, or perhaps they exist, but you're using the wrong lure or bait to attract them. I've noticed there are different strokes for different folks, but I think it's more important to be aware of the water you're fishing in.

When it comes to dating, a woman may be desiring a godly man (fish), but it'll be hard to find him in a nightclub (water). The only kind of man she's likely to attract at the club is a barracuda who wants to party all the time. Or a woman may come across as an "easy catch" by wearing seductive clothing or not dressing modestly. Godly men avoid her while she attracts men who only want to take her to bed and not make a commitment to her.

It's been said over and over that there's nothing like a well-dressed man, well-groomed man, well-mannered man! Now, on the other hand, ladies, you can't put demands on the man if you're not willing to do the same because every man wants a beautiful woman who's very presentable, soft, sensitive, and sexy all at the same time.

Every woman should look like a woman, talk like a woman, walk like a woman, so, please dress like a woman. It's been said that people address you by the way you dress, so you can be classy without being trashy. When men and women present themselves correctly, it's very inviting to the opposite sex.

APPLICATION QUESTIONS

1. What kind of bait are you using?

_____
_____
_____
_____

2. Where are you fishing?

   _____
   _____
   _____
   _____
   _____

3. What qualities are you looking for in a mate? Do you have some of these qualities?

   _____
   _____
   _____
   _____
   _____

4. Why aren't many people successful at finding a mate?

   _____
   _____
   _____
   _____
   _____

CHAPTER 8

PRIVATE PROPERTY

I recently noticed a sign while hunting that read "Absolutely no hunting on this property. It is a private property. All violators will be prosecuted." And in big red lettering, it said, "Please stay out. Stay off property!" Some signs even read, "Reserved for Special Hunters Only. Sorry but this is not KFC. You don't get legs, thighs, breast here. This is private property for now!"

Many people make the mistake of giving away the goods for free. Why buy the cow if you can get the milk for free? Why would a man marry you if you give him all the marital benefits without a long-term commitment? Our members or body parts should be considered private property just like those signs I saw when I went hunting. They're private because only your God-ordained spouse is supposed to have access to it.

Romans 6:12-13 says, "Let not sin therefore reign in your mortal body, that ye should obey it in the lusts thereof. Neither yield ye your members as instruments of unrighteousness unto sin: but yield yourselves unto God, as those that are alive from the dead, and your members as instruments of righteousness unto God."

No sin should reign in our private properties. We are human, and we have desires, but we need to learn how to submit those desires unto the Lord. Sin should not control our lives, but we should be fully filled of the Spirit of God. We don't want our members or body parts to be full of lust. Lust can never be satisfied. Once you get a taste of something, no amount will be able to quench your thirst for it. You'll just keep eating until you destroy yourself. This is what the enemy wants because his job is to kill, steal, and destroy us (John 10:10).

Our body parts should be used as instruments of righteous. You can yield your body unto God by making a vow to Him to practice abstinence. You can resist the enemy, and he will flee (James 4:7). You must fast (abstaining from foods) to break strongholds of lust. You need to take time to meditate on the Word of God because it's your spiritual sword (Ephesians 6:17) to fight the enemy. You need to pray so you won't be led into temptation (Matthew 26:41). If you're weak or are having difficulties with a trespasser on your private property, ask God to strengthen you. Make the decision to give no more people illegal access, no more trespassers, and to keep your property locked until that special hunter (spouse) comes along.

The next time someone wants to violate your rules, remind yourself of that sign that says, "Absolutely no hunting on this property. It is private property. All violators will be prosecuted. Please stay out. Stay off property!"

APPLICATION QUESTIONS

1. What is the significance of valuing our members as private property?

2. What ways can a person yield their members as instruments of righteousness?

3. What are the dangers of allowing anyone to have access to private property?

4. How can you apply the term "Private Property" to your own life?

_____
_____
_____
_____
_____

CHAPTER 9

DESTINY DATING VS. SHOTGUN DATING

There are two types of dating styles: destiny and shotgun. In destiny dating you focus on the target. In shotgun dating you try to hit whatever is available.[4] In destiny dating you aren't dating a ton of people, but are more focused on purpose. In shotgun dating, you're dating many people at one time, either online or in person and hanging out with them.

The difference between a bullet and a shell is that shells are filled with tiny rolled balls. When you shoot a shotgun, it spreads everywhere to increase the chance of you hitting the target. It's great for hunting, but it's terrible for dating.

Shotgun dating is not good because it creates a mentality that lacks commitment or "sticking to it power". There are way too many choices in shotgun dating and you can be threatened by too many choices. You'll end up confused, not even knowing what you want.

1 Corinthians 14:33 says, "For God is not the author of confusion, but of peace, as in all churches of the saints."

If it's not God's plan for you right now, don't be coerced by culture pressure. Just because everyone else is doing something doesn't mean God is pleased with it. Don't be conformed to the world's way of dating but to God's way. The Bible warns us that to be a friend of the world make us an enemy to God (James 4:4). We need to be very careful not to follow carnal advice.

We must have discipled restraint when it comes to dating. We need to exercise self-control, and we need a laser-sharp focus, which is destiny dating. Destiny dating involves practicing abstinence from sexual activities that promote holiness.

1 Peter 1:16 says, "Because it is written, Be ye holy; for I am holy."

The sacrifice is worth the prize. Not easy, but worth it.

APPLICATION QUESTIONS

1. What are the differences between destiny dating and shotgun dating?

_____

_____

_____

_____

2. How is shotgun dating risky?

_____

_____

_____

3. What are the pros to destiny dating?

_____
_____
_____
_____
_____

4. What steps can be taken to prevent you from shotgun dating?

_____
_____
_____
_____
_____

CHAPTER 10

LOOKING FOR LOVE IN ALL THE WRONG PLACES

I've spoken to many singles in my career, trying to encourage them along the way. After surviving multiple relationships, many of which end in divorce or separation or end painfully for whatever reason, are left with the big question in their mind. Does true love really exist? Can I really be happy? Is there really a special person out there just for me? Or is all this love stuff just a myth?

I have some good news for you. True love is real, and it does exist. Now, finding it may be a challenge, but it's out there. I remember one young lady saying to me, "I only attract trashy men." I simply replied, "Stop hanging out at the dump."

There are four simple guidelines to follow when looking for love:

1. Don't lower your standards for anyone.
2. Set goals in your dating.
3. Make sure the goals are realistic goals and not over the top.
4. Be careful in giving out too much too quickly.

Let's discuss guideline number one. Anytime you lower your standards, you're compromising. You're settling for less because you're being impatient or don't believe in waiting for God's best for your life. James 1:4 says, "But let patience have her perfect work, that ye may be perfect and entire, wanting nothing." When we wait on God, we will be satisfied.

When standards are lowered, anything goes. Proverbs 25:28 says, "He that hath no rule over his own spirit is like a city that is broken down, and without walls." A person might decide to date an unbeliever (we'll discuss this in another chapter) or a person might choose to date someone with more red flags than a May Day parade but choose to overlook them because they want to have a relationship.

The number two guideline is setting goals. You must know what you want. You must have a vision. Proverbs 29:18 says, "Where there is no vision, the people perish." Many times, they are in such a rush to satisfy their out of control emotions that they pick up the first relationship they see. The purpose of setting goals is to determine if that person is right for you. And in order to be successful in setting goals, you must write your vision.

Habakkuk 2:2-3 says, "And the Lord answered me, and said, Write the vision, and make it plain upon tables, that he may run that readeth it. For the vision is yet for an appointed time, but at the end it shall speak, and not lie: though it tarry, wait for it; because it will surely come, it will not tarry."

The third guideline is making sure your goals are realistic. We'll discuss more of this in a later chapter, but many dating goals are over the top or unrealistic. A woman may want a man with no kids, but she has six of them; she may want a man with a great job, but she can barely keep one; she may want a faithful man, but she is unfaithful. I could go on, but it's important to remember that you must be able to attract and match what you want and then put in the time to get there.

The last guideline is being careful not to give too much too quick. In today's generation, people want microwave relationships, unwilling to put the time and effort into creating a slow-cooked relationship that will stand the test of time. Many times, they are in such a rush to fill their emotional bellies that they don't cook anything at home, choosing to pick up whatever relationship they can at the local relationship fast-food drive-thru. Seeking nothing more than instant gratification, they'll meet someone online one day, and the next day they're talking about being in love and moving in together.

What's the rush? It's impossible to know everything you need to know about another person in a short amount of time. Relationships are ever-evolving and ever-growing. Take your time and get to know the person you're dating. When you give out too much too quickly, it screams "I'm desperate!" and will push people away from you. Or worse, you could end up being used for a while and then dropped like a hot potato.

Can you really live happily ever after? Is it possible to strike gold? Yes, true love does exist. You've just got to stop looking in the wrong places. Pray and ask God to send the right person into your life.

APPLICATION QUESTIONS

1. What steps can you take to ensure that you will never look for love in the wrong places?

   _____
   _____
   _____
   _____
   _____

2. What are some guidelines you can apply when looking for love?

   _____
   _____
   _____
   _____
   _____

3. What are your goals when it comes to dating?

   _____
   _____
   _____
   _____
   _____

4. What is the importance of setting guidelines in dating?

_____
_____
_____
_____
_____

CHAPTER 11

DON'T PREHEAT THE OVEN IF YOUR NOT COOKING ANYTHING

Don't bait the hook if you're not going fishing. There's nothing like hormone explosions to destroy a relationship. For instance, there are women who dress in clothes that are too revealing and then wonder why men approach them sexually. If you're preheating the oven and you're not cooking, then this is nothing but seductive deception because you're offering an illusion. Playing with people's hearts like this is a dangerous game. God wants His children to be honest. When we stay true to God's heart, our ways are secure.

Proverbs 10:9 says, "He that walketh uprightly walketh surely: but he that perverteth his ways shall be known."

There are questions that must be answered when you're ready to cook in a preheated oven. In other words, when you're ready to date and want to eliminate the fools and the counterfeits, these eight questions must be answered:

Let's Investigate

1. Are both of you saved, single, and sanctified?
2. Are you gainfully employed?
3. Do you have a good credit score?
4. Check out his/her family tree. You are the fruit of somebody's root.
5. How many children do you have? Even the ones you don't claim?
6. Do you or did you previously pay child support?
7. Are you true to your word? Are they?
8. Can you be trusted? Can they?

Question number one: dating someone who's saved, single, and sanctified is God's will for your life. You want to date someone who's saved because they most likely have a relationship with Jesus Christ. You must date someone who's single, not someone who's married but separated. God will never give you someone else's spouse.

Proverbs 10:22 says, "The blessing of the Lord, it maketh rich, and he addeth no sorrow with it." God's blessings have no trouble with it. You want to date someone who has been sanctified because you don't want to date someone full of lust, perversion, anger, pride, and other such sins. Sanctification means the state of growing in divine grace as a result of Christian commitment after baptism or conversion.[5] In other words, the person is becoming more Christ-like and holy. You never want to date someone who'll cause you to stumble in your walk with God.

Question number two: there is nothing wrong with asking someone if they are gainfully employed. This means they have a great job, are not making only minimum wage, and are not in between jobs. They have consistent work.

You don't want to date someone who leeches off you. Finances are one of the top reasons why people divorce. Women want to marry men who are great providers. Some folks settle and overlook this issue only to regret it later.

Question number three: asking someone if they have a good credit score is a sense of security. When your credit score is good, you can get approved for almost anything: house, car, furniture, appliances, and anything else you may buy on credit. This is an indication how responsible a person is because they worked to build up their credit over the years. It also shows they can pay their bills on time. You want to marry someone who's responsible, so you won't come up short every month when the bills are due.

Question number four: looking into their family history is vital. You need to know if they have abandonment issues or alcoholism in their family. Was their father abusive toward their mother? Did they come from a broken family? Does anyone have mental issues? As the old saying goes, the apple doesn't fall too far from the tree. If the person has some issues in their past, make sure they're fully delivered and committed to God before you two proceed down the altar.

Question number five: dating someone with children can be challenging. You might have to deal with baby momma drama or a crazy jealous ex. It takes a special grace from God to have blended families or a family that includes children of a previous relationship or marriage. The children may give you a hard time because you aren't their biological parent. This can be stressful on any relationship. Are you willing to love and care for those children like they're your own? Many families are destroyed because of a dysfunctional family unit.

Question six: when you date someone who pays child support, you need to realize that's money that could be spent on your future family but won't be. If that person doesn't pay their child support, that could affect you too. The IRS can garnish your joint tax return or joint bank accounts. Your partner can go to jail or get their license revoked. Are you willing to stand by this person if the worst happens? Do you want to date someone who's negligent in paying child support when there's a child in the world depending on this income? If this is the way that person is behaving now, what makes you think they'll act differently with you?

Question seven: you need to know if the person is true to their word. Nothing is worse than dating a liar. The Bible says the devil is the father of all lies (John 8:44). You don't want to date a child of the devil. They'll lie about anything: where they were, what they ate, where they work, how much they make. At the end of the day, it's like you're dating a complete stranger because you don't know if what they told you is true. Plus, you want to date someone who's reliable and can be depended on if you were to ever go through a trial. There's nothing more comforting than knowing that someone has your back and is in your corner. We all need a great support system.

Question eight: can the person be trusted? In other words, are they faithful and loyal? Will they cheat on you behind your back? Will they turn against you? Can you trust them with your deepest secrets or will they try to make you look bad to make themselves look better? Proverbs 11:13 says, "A talebearer revealeth secrets: but he that is of a faithful spirit concealeth the matter." Can you trust them to stick around for the long haul or are they just playing games?

APPLICATION QUESTIONS

1. What are the dangers of dressing provocative while looking for a mate?

2. What are some questions that must be discussed before getting involved in a relationship?

3. Why is it important to trust a person while in a relationship?"

4. How does asking the right questions eliminate the counterfeit relationships?

_____
_____
_____
_____
_____

CHAPTER 12

UNREALISTIC EXPECTATIONS

Although I believe a person should have standards when it comes to dating, we all need to have realistic expectations. We need to be careful to not put upon others that which we aren't able or willing to perform ourselves. Yes, everyone wants the best relationship, but at the same time, let's not set the standard so high that no one is able to reach it. For example, only dating millionaires who own luxury houses and cars with no children may be an unrealistic expectation. You could very well miss out on what God has for you because of holding unrealistic expectations so high they are unobtainable for most people.

I admire the fact that you want and desire the very best, and you aspire to be the best, but let's be real about it. Yes, by all means, set goals and pursue your vision. I personally encourage that, but on the other hand, make sure your goals are obtainable and doable.

James 1:22 says, "But be ye doers of the word, and not hearers only, deceiving your own selves."

I've seen so many people who seem to be overachievers, and when things don't work out, it feels like their whole world comes crashing down on them. What should have been a wonderful journey has now become a major setback. Enjoy your journey one day at a time. Learn to embrace the moment, slow down, and relax! Take a chill pill and go with the flow. Don't chase life; let it find you, and it will. If something is meant to be, God has a way of connecting the dots.

Psalm 37:23 says, "The steps of a good man are ordered by the Lord: and he delighteth in his way."

Also make sure you're not demanding more than you're willing to give yourself. It's not fair for you to present a list of items or demands of over-the-top stuff; if the tables were turned, would you be receptive of what you're demanding or expecting from the opposite sex?

APPLICATION QUESTIONS

1. What are your expectations in dating? Are they realistic?

    _____
    _____
    _____
    _____
    _____

2. Why are realistic expectations important?

    _____
    _____
    _____
    _____
    _____

3. What are some consequences of having unrealistic expectations?

4. Why is it important to perform the same demands we put on others?

CHAPTER 13

AVOID ABUSIVE RELATIONSHIPS

The thing that hurts about abusive relationships is when you realize you're in one, you feel tricked and deceived. Most abusive relationships don't start out with a black eye or bruises all over your body. Most start out too good to be true. But slowly, your partner may begin to subtly blame you for things beyond your control or pick at your faults. This may evolve into full-blown verbal or physical abuse.

An abusive relationship drains you and strips you of your dignity. It kills your self-worth, leaving you feeling trapped and miserable before you even realize the signs. Regardless of whether you suffer from emotional abuse, physical abuse, or verbal abuse, it's hard to comprehend that someone you love and claims to love you could victimize you. Sometimes your partner may not even realize what they're doing is wrong. I felt that after speaking with so many who've experienced the trauma of abuse, it was important to include this chapter because of people presently living in an abusive situation or those who have come out of one.

Here are a few signs of an abusive situation:

1. Humiliation—Starts out with verbal stabbing and jabbing in private, and then becomes yelling and screaming in public. It's meant to make you submissive and controlled in public, so you harken to their power.
2. Verbal Insults—You or your partner may lose your cool in an argument, but it never excuses name calling and foul language. Verbal abuse can range anywhere from insulting your looks, your worth, or your intelligence. The main goal is to destroy your self-esteem.
3. Physical Violence—Physical abuse never starts with a busted lip or a black eye. It starts with the spirit of intimidation: hand raised, a sinister stare in the eyes, or a quick slap to get your attention. They are constantly trying to break you down.
4. Walking on eggshells to avoid disappointing your partner—they require check-in times; they want to know where you are and who you're with at all times, and they constantly keep tabs on you. This is harassment.
5. You find yourself apologizing when you've done nothing wrong—You're left feeling stupid when you're totally innocent.
6. Partner loving one minute and hateful the next—Close one minute but distant and unavailable the next. They deny being withdrawn, so they make you suffer. They want you to get back into their good graces.
7. Putting you down and belittling you with degrading comments—Their goal is to make you feel like no one else would want you except for them, so you'll stay with them and put up with their abuse.

8. Withholding affection to punish you—They want you to feel what they feel. They'll lash out at you and punish you for other's mistakes. They'll take out their frustrations on you.
9. Always feeling sorry for them, although they hurt you—they have you blaming yourself for their mistakes and outbursts. You'll ignore their faults and take ownership of them.

God wants you to prosper in every area of your life, including your relationships. He didn't create you to be anyone's punching bag. He wants you to be whole. He never wants you to stay in an abusive relationship because it could be dangerous. Many people have died due to domestic abuse. If you're a victim of abuse, take the following steps for your journey to wholeness.

1. **Seek the Lord and ask Him for discernment.**
   Psalm 119:66 says, "Teach me good judgment (discernment) and knowledge: for I have believed thy commandments."

2. **Ask the Lord for protection from the evil one (abuser).**
   2 Thessalonians 3:3 says, "But the Lord is faithful, who shall stablish you, and keep you from evil."

3. **Pray to see yourself as God sees you.**
   Psalm 139:14 says, "I will praise thee; for I am fearfully and wonderfully made: marvelous are thy works; and that my soul knoweth right well."

4. **Pray that God will break the cycle (stronghold) of abusive relationships.**
   2 Corinthians 10:4 says, "For the weapons of our warfare are not carnal, but mighty through God to the pulling down of strong holds."

5. **Pray for the courage to leave.**
   Joshua 1:9 says, "Have not I commanded thee? Be strong and of a good courage; be not afraid, neither be thou dismayed: for the Lord thy God is with thee whithersoever thou goest."

APPLICATION QUESTIONS

1. Describe an abusive relationship?

   _____
   _____
   _____
   _____
   _____

2. What are some of the signs of an abusive relationship?

   _____
   _____
   _____
   _____
   _____

3. What are some dangers of staying in an abusive relationship?

_____
_____
_____
_____
_____

4. What are some steps to take on a journey to wholeness?

_____
_____
_____
_____
_____

CHAPTER 14

LIVE-INS ARE FILL-INS

Too often couples are lured into living together, which, by the way, should be a wonderful privilege and a very nice benefit reserved for those who are married. These couples follow the ways of the world when it comes to dating and enjoy the benefits without the responsibility and commitment. They think that living together is "taking their relationship to the next level" but ignore the fact that they are in sin.

They may even feel like living together will help them save money, so they can get married later. This lie is a temporary fix, not a permanent solution, and it's one of the ways the enemy deceives us. The devil loves to plant ideas that seem great but will cost us in the end.

1 Thessalonians 4:3-5 says, "For this is the will of God, even your sanctification, that ye should abstain from fornication: That every one of you should know how to possess his vessel in sanctification and honour; Not in the lust of concupiscence, even as the Gentiles which know not God."

God wants us to be holy and stay away from sexual sin. He wants us to live in a way that glorifies Him. Does living together with the person you're dating glorify God? Don't live like worldly people who don't know God.

1 Corinthians 7:1-2 says, "Now concerning the things whereof ye wrote unto me: It is good for a man not to touch a woman. Nevertheless, to avoid fornication, let every man have his own wife, and let every woman have her own husband."

The Apostle Paul said that it's good for a man not to touch a woman. The reason is that it can lead to fornication. Touching can lead to kissing. Kissing can lead to fornication. If you live with someone then they can see your most intimate moments, like when you're sleeping or when you're in the bathroom. These intimate moments belong within a marriage.

1 Corinthians 7:8-9 says, "I say therefore to the unmarried and widows, it is good for them if they abide even as I. But if they cannot contain, let them marry: for it is better to marry than to burn."

The Apostle Paul said that if a person can't exercise self-control concerning sex, then they should marry. It's impossible to live with someone whom you're attracted to and not be intimate with them. Living together or shacking up is playing with fire and sin. My dear friends, if you believe that it will one day enhance your marriage, you are sadly mistaken. It's okay to plan for the future, but not to the point that we forfeit our destiny. Fornicators will not make it to heaven.

1 Corinthians 6:9-10 says, "Know ye not that the unrighteous shall not inherit the kingdom of God? Be not deceived: neither fornicators, nor idolaters, nor adulterers, nor effeminate, nor abusers of themselves with mankind, nor thieves, nor covetous, nor drunkards, nor revilers, nor extortioners, shall inherit the kingdom of God."

APPLICATION QUESTIONS

1. What are the consequences of living together before marriage?

   _____
   _____
   _____
   _____
   _____

2. How are people lured to live together before marriage?

   _____
   _____
   _____
   _____
   _____

3. How can you ensure that you won't live with the person you are dating before marriage?

   _____
   _____
   _____
   _____
   _____

4. In what ways are people deceived when it comes to living together before marriage?

_____
_____
_____
_____
_____

CHAPTER 15

BELIEVERS DON'T MARRY UNBELIEVERS

For a Christian to marry an unbeliever is a violation of the will of God. God warns us against this sin. In 2 Corinthians 6:14, God said to be not unequally yoked with unbelievers. It's never the will of God for a Christian to marry an unbeliever. Before you are tempted to do so, don't accept a date or become too close or too attached to an unbeliever. Learn to say no before it's too late. In other words, don't even go there!

I've witnessed good Christians crossing the line to reach the forbidden fruit over and over again, thinking they can convert them. Sorry, but that's a recipe for a catastrophe. Most of those marriages end up in divorce or in-house separation with a divided home where one honors God and is faithful to the house of God, while the other one doesn't believe at all. It doesn't stop there. In many instances, the unbelieving spouse draws the believing spouse away from God, and then suddenly, the children are affected and left feeling that they have to choose. All because it started out the wrong way.

Some Questions to Ask Before You Say "I Do"

There are plenty of questions to ask early in the relationship to help ensure a good fit, but let's be honest; most couples won't. Secrets lead to disappointments down the road, so if you don't deal with issues before marriage, get ready to deal with them later. It may seem a little awkward at the beginning, but it's important in a relationship and in a marriage to make sure you are on one accord and on the same page. Don't be reckless.

1. How do you deal with difficulties?
It could determine the success of your relationship. Are you willing to confront your issues so you're able to conquer them? Or do you suppress them or sweep them under the rug? You may try to hide it, but it's still there. Why should we discuss these issues now? Because every marriage will have challenges, misunderstandings, and bumps in the road. But through respectful dialogue, you can work through anything.

2. Are you over your Ex?
It's a hard question to ask, but it must be asked because it can and will affect your relationship. If you still have a soul tie with an ex, that soul tie needs to be broken or you'll go into a new relationship with a divided heart, not really giving that person all of you because part of you remains with someone else.
I've heard horrible stories on how many exes have tormented one another, not wanting them anymore, but they still can't stand the fact that they're seeing someone else. Break all ties, loose them, and let them go! Let's be clear, your ex can be an ex-wife, ex-husband, ex-

boyfriend, or an ex-girlfriend. The last thing your new relationship needs is the baggage of an old partnership or relationship. They are your ex for a reason.

3. How will we celebrate holidays, especially if you both come from a different religious background?
For instance, if you married a Jehovah's Witness, be prepared to not celebrate birthdays or Christmas. Are you willing to compromise or be flexible to support their beliefs? Do you want to risk your relationship with Jesus Christ and put Him on the back burner to celebrate a holiday that goes against Him? Will you celebrate holidays that originated from a demonic beginning?

4. Is my debt your debt? Will you bail out one another?
You must discuss financial issues and money matters. Are you willing to budget? Are you disciplined in your spending? Are you going to have a joint bank account? Who will be in charge of paying the bills? Have you ever declared bankruptcy? Are you opposed to saving money? Do you have a problem releasing the checkbook to the one who knows how to balance the books? Finances are crucial! Money has split a myriad of marriages.

APPLICATION QUESTIONS

1. What are the dangers of a believer dating an un-believer?

2. What are some questions to ask before you say "I do"?

3. How are children affected if a believer and non-believer get married?

4. Why is it important to discuss financial issues before you say "I do"?

_____
_____
_____
_____
_____

CHAPTER 16

LYING LOVERS

Lying lovers are the game players. They break all the rules; they know what to say and how to say it; and they know when to say it. They are ego strokers, and they are the silver-tongued master manipulators. Sorry, they don't have to be fine; they just have a good line. You really must guard your heart. The weak and the vulnerable fall prey to the lying lovers. Full of flattery targeting the simple, they can detect your insecurities. They tell every target the same thing.

Psalm 52:2-3 says, "The tongue deviseth mischiefs; like a sharp razor, working deceitfully. Thou lovest evil more than good; and lying rather than to speak righteousness. Selah."

They have no intention of committing or entering a lifetime relationship. They're selfish and self-serving and are all about themselves. Their tongues are like a serpent, simply poison.

Psalm 140:3 says, "They have sharpened their tongues like a serpent; adders' poison is under their lips. Selah."

Don't waste your words on them when they deserve your silence. They're not affected by breakup because they have no intention of staying with you anyway. Lose them and let them be—NOW! Don't chase them; replace them. Focus on God so you can have the strength you need to not give in to their tactics. They're being used of the enemy and need to be delivered.

James 4:7 says, "Submit yourselves therefore to God. Resist the devil, and he will flee from you."

Breakups hurt, and they hurt really bad. Then the ugly words that are being used can destroy your self-esteem. That makes you feel like you have something to prove, and that's certainly the wrong attitude to embrace. You now feel you need to prove you're totally over him or her, and you have just replaced them for revenge. That's a sign of immaturity on your part, and while it's meant to hurt them, it'll only end up hurting you and the new person they're dating.

So, after a breakup, focus on you. Learn to grow as a person getting healed and whole. Then move on with your life. Here are a few lies told by lying lovers:

1. I love you.

Lying lovers will tell you they love you to manipulate and control you in order to get what they want from you. Once they get what they want, they kick you to the curb. Women love sweet words, and they often cross the line into sexual immorality when a man tells them they love them. They'll often try other ways to express their love monetarily. Beware of the enemy. Pray that ravenous wolves in sheep's clothing will be revealed.

2. They're just a friend.

Lying lovers will tell you that the lady or man you just saw was merely a friend, but your gut feeling says otherwise. Don't ignore the red flags. Pay attention to body language. God will never put you in a relationship with someone who will walk all over your heart. He wants the best for you.

3. I'm sorry.

Lying lovers will tell you that they're sorry and that they'll change just so they can keep you around. Don't fall for it. It's hard to gain trust back once it's broken. Stop the cycle of broken promises and empty nothings. You need to refuse to not deal with it anymore and just walk away. Cut all ties.

4. I love God.

Don't be deceived. Lying lovers will pretend they love God just to get close to you. They'll go to church with you as an act while secretly plotting their next move on you. They pretend to pray to God, but they only prey on innocent victims. They're just a huge phony.

5. I need to work late.

Lying lovers will say they need to work late so they can chat and hang out with your replacement. They'll tell you this so you won't bother them while they do their dirty work. If you notice a change, take heed. God may be giving you a heads up, so you can get out.

APPLICATION QUESTIONS

1. What does the term "lying lovers" mean?

2. What steps can a person take to prevent them from being a prey to a "lying lover"?

3. What are some lies that "lying lovers" tell?

4. What are some of the consequences of ignoring the warnings signs?

CHAPTER 17

BURDEN OF BAGGAGE

Emotional baggage can be detrimental. It's very important that you discern it before you're knee deep into it. You must sort out your emotions before they worsen over time and handicap your ability to love someone else. In a previous chapter, I mentioned the danger of rebound relationships. Especially after divorce, because divorce can be a traumatic event. Maybe you've spent years with a person, and now you need time to heal and move on. Here are a few steps to follow that will help you heal from your baggage.

1. **Identify your baggage. Don't act like it is not there.**

Do you have unresolved feelings of love for your ex-spouse or another past love? If so, it's time to confront those feelings so that cloud over your head can vanish. You need to decree and declare right now that it is over! Mean it when you say it and then move on.

Job 22:28 says, "Thou shalt also decree a thing, and it shall be established unto thee: and the light shall shine upon thy ways."

Don't allow resentment and bitterness to set in. It may have caused an emotional scar, but scars do heal. Don't try to put a bandage over your scars but give it all to God!

1 Peter 5:7 says, "Casting all your care upon him; for he careth for you."

Remember, your pain will serve a purpose. Joseph went through betrayal when his brothers sold him into slavery (Genesis 37:18-36). He went through persecution when his master's wife accused him of wanting to sleep with her. He spent years in prison for a crime he didn't commit (Genesis 39:13-20).

Years later, he saw his brothers again, and he wept (Genesis 42:24). It was his way of coping with the pain, but he let it go. He realized that his pain had a purpose.

Genesis 50:20 says, "But as for you, ye thought evil against me; but God meant it unto good, to bring to pass, as it is this day, to save much people alive."

He didn't get bitter, he got better. He eliminated his emotional baggage, and you can too.

2. Do you have a strong desire to see your ex fail?

This is a strong sign you're carrying some emotional baggage. If you want them to suffer because you're suffering, then it's also a sign that you haven't released or let go of that person. When you release the baggage and forgive that person, then you really don't care who they're with or who they're dating. In fact, when you've forgiven them, you want them to be happy and do well.

Ephesians 4:32 says, "And be ye kind one to another, tenderhearted, forgiving one another, even as God for Christ's sake hath forgiven you."

Show your ex the love of God, and don't allow the enemy to get underneath your skin. Pray for them.

Matthew 5:44 says, "But I say unto you, love your enemies, bless them that curse you, do good to them that hate you, and pray for them which despitefully use you, and persecute you."

You want to have a pure heart before God because that's what He looks at. So, it's time for you to eliminate that baggage.

3. Accept your past for what it is and realize you can't change it.

It's time for you to be truthfully honest with yourself and make peace with yourself. Pay attention to the warning signs. If your heart is saying one thing and your head is saying another, please...please...please don't ignore it! When you're arguing with your ex in your head, and they're nowhere around, that's a bad sign. When you hear about them breaking up again with someone different and you are happy, that's a bad sign!

So, what do you do? Well, it's time for confession. It's okay to acknowledge that you're struggling in this area, and you feel as if your options are endless, but remember to take the time you need to get your healing.

There's no specific time frame. There's no "one size fits all." You're done when you're done. You'll come out stronger and wiser, and you'll rise to the next level because now you're mentally stable and focused. No longer on again off again, but back on track. So, go ahead and unload all the emotional baggage, so that when God grants you your petition, you'll be ready to walk into your destiny! Remember, everybody has baggage, regardless of who they are. The only thing that really matters is how you handle it.

Don't allow the enemy to cause you shame and condemnation (Romans 8:1). God forgave you; now, forgive yourself. The past doesn't have to last. Learn from the mistakes and become a better person.

APPLICATION QUESTIONS

1. What is the danger of bringing baggage into a relationship?

   _____
   _____
   _____
   _____

2. What's some emotional baggage that needs to be addressed before anyone enters into a relationship?

   _____
   _____
   _____
   _____
   _____

3. How do you know that you're ready to enter a new relationship?

_____
_____
_____
_____
_____

4. What is the significance of forgiving your ex and releasing your past?

_____
_____
_____
_____
_____

CHAPTER 18

STAYING FAITHFUL IN THE FIELD

The story of Ruth and Naomi is such a wonderful story in the Bible. It's one of sacrifice, love, and endurance. While Ruth sacrificed and put her life on hold to meet the needs of others, we see her unselfish acts of kindness. As a result, her life ends with joy, peace, love, and happiness. She was simply working in a field faithfully, not looking for a mate. Content, comfortable, and staying focused. I believe every single woman should read this story; it will certainly encourage you, help you, and strengthen you along the way.

While Ruth was faithfully focused on her mother-in-law, being careful about all her needs, God had someone looking out for her also (Ruth 2). I truly believe that what God has for you is perfectly just for you. I also believe that what you make happen for others, God will also make it happen for you. As you continue to read this chapter, I'll show you steps to Ruth's blessings she received in her life.

1. She was first faithful in her field (Ruth 2:7,17). I want to encourage you to stay in your field. Stay faithful and stay focused. Stop playing the field and start praying in the field!

God honors faithfulness. The question is, what field are you working in? While Ruth was faithful in the field, she finds Boaz. Boaz is the owner of the field she was working in (Ruth 2:3). She had no idea he was interested in her. You never know who's watching you or inquiring about you. After he asked questions about Ruth, they told him how faithful she'd been to her mother-in-law and how she'd been helping her (Ruth 2:5-6,11).

2. She is hidden in the field. God allowed the right man to see her at the right time.

When a man finds a woman, he finds a good thing, and obtains favor from God (Proverbs 18:22). Little did Ruth know that God was setting her up for one of the greatest blessings of her life. Some of you are reading this book and are probably wondering when your time will come. You may be closer than you think. Ruth had no idea she was being noticed or discussed in private. God knows how to amplify you. Your potential mate will notice you out of all the women in the field, out of all the women in the office, out of all the women in the factory, out of all the women on the team, out of all the women in the church. He will choose you!

3. Ruth's faithfulness to Naomi caused her to have great favor with Boaz.

Ruth found favor in Boaz's sight because she was faithful to her mother in law, Naomi. When a man finds a woman, he finds a good thing, and favor with God (Proverbs 18:22). Little did she know God was setting her up for one of the greatest blessings of her life. She left everything familiar to go with Naomi to an unfamiliar place. God also favored her for what she did (Ruth 2:10-12). Ruth was well taken care of while she worked in the field. She ate until she was full (Ruth 2:14) and Boaz allowed her to gather as much grain as she wanted without reprimand (Ruth 2:15-16).

4. Ruth got the fella. She was able to embrace the blessing because she humbled herself and followed wise counsel.

She probably seemed like the least likely person to get remarried. Her husband had died, and she was just trying to make sure her mother in-law would be okay. She was noble in her efforts, and she had realistic expectations. Boaz told her that she didn't need to look for a young, rich, or poor man to marry (Ruth 3:10). She followed Naomi's plans to let Boaz know that she was interested (Ruth 3:1-9). She washed, put on perfume, and went down to the threshing floor. She watched Boaz without him knowing it. After Boaz ate his dinner and fell asleep, she uncovered his feet and laid down. This was symbolic of a request for provision and protection of marriage.

5. Boaz did what he had to do to marry Ruth.

Another gentleman or kinsman was next in line to marry Ruth. Yet the kinsman wasn't willing to carry out her dead husband's name so it wouldn't be cut off from his brethren. However, Boaz was willing, and he went down to the gates of the city and followed the necessary protocols (Ruth 4:3-10). He married Ruth and she conceived (Ruth 4:13). The Messiah would come through her bloodline (Ruth 4:17).

She was faithful in the field. While she was working (faithful) in the field, favor showed up and found her. When you're faithful in your field God favors you. Then her fella shows up and then everything points toward her future, which ended up being her family.

APPLICATION QUESTIONS

1. What is the significance of the story of Ruth when it comes to being faithful in the field?

_____
_____
_____
_____
_____

2. In what ways does God honor faithfulness?

_____
_____
_____
_____
_____

3. What is your field and how can you be faithful?

_____
_____
_____
_____

4. What steps did Ruth take in order to receive the blessings on her life?

_____
_____
_____
_____

CHAPTER 19

COMMITTED RELATIONSHIPS

Commitment in a relationship is an agreement between two people, not only one person making all the decisions. Commitment can also be defined as a promise to do or give something; a promise to be loyal to someone or something; the attitude of someone who works very hard to do or support something.[7] When you judge the progress of a relationship, it helps you make future commitments in a relationship. Here are a few pointers to show your level of commitment in a relationship.

1. **The love and the respect you have for one another shows your level of commitment in a relationship.**

When you have love and respect in a commitment relationship, you honor each other's boundaries no matter what. You also support each other's values, feelings, and needs. Lastly, you support each other's interests, hobbies, careers, and more.

However, to ignore the dreams, visions, and views of the other, it's a sign of selfishness. Love is not selfish (1 Corinthians 13:5). How can you tell if there is a level of commitment when it comes to love and respect? Growing in love and caring for one another, likes and dislikes, are very good signs, but compromising on your individual standards is not healthy. Being honest, open, and upfront with no hidden agenda also shows your level of commitment in a relationship.

There should be no secrets, and you should be able to share your feelings and share yourself in the presence of your partner. This is a sign of being totally committed. Apart from this, you've been honest about your past and you've truthfully told your partner your hopes for your future; that's another sign of commitment. You don't want anything to get between you and your partner, nor anything that will hurt the relationship later when things come up from the past.

2. Another sign of commitment is that you are loyal in every aspect of your relationship and the promises you've made to each other.

Coupled with honesty, loyalty plays a huge part in your relationship. Loyalty is staying faithful to the promises and to the vows you've made to each other. Loyalty is sticking with the person through thick and thin. You'll be by their side through the trials and help them become better in life. You won't do things behind their back, flirt with other people, or have emotional intimacy with someone else. When you're loyal, then there's no doubt you are committed.

3. **Another key component is spending time with one another and enjoying one another's company to the fullest. That shows them that you are committed to him or her.**

You should have feelings about one another and be willing to fulfill one another's desires. I've found this to be one of the most fulfilling aspects of a relationship. You'll always find time or make time for something or someone you love. It's during these times where you can reconnect by talking and dating. Spending time together can help strengthen your relationship and form a closeness you share with no other person.

4. **The willingness to stick to it, or as we call it, "Staying Power!" This is another sign that you're committed.**

There's no feeling worse than the spirit of abandonment or of easily bailing out. Life's not always a bed of roses. There will be times when you'll go through things—ups and downs—and your relationship will be tested, but when the dust settles and the smoke clears, if you're still there, then that is a great sign of commitment. When you're still able to support one another through it all that makes for a great committed relationship.

Remember, commitment in a relationship means devotion on both sides. Make sure you play your part, and never demand from your partner what you're unwilling to give in return.

Always keep in in mind that you both are striving for the same goal, and there will be storms along the way. If at any time you feel your commitment weakening, that's the time to batten down the hatches and stay the course!

APPLICATION QUESTIONS

1. What is a committed relationship?

2. What are the signs of a committed relationship?

3. Why should someone judge the process of their relationship?

4. If you are in a relationship, evaluate it. Are you and your partner committed to one another? What areas need to be strengthened?

_____
_____
_____
_____
_____

CHAPTER 20

THE IMPORTANCE OF COMMUNICATION

Communication is vital in any relationship. In order to maintain a healthy relationship, you must effectively communicate. Communication to a relationship is like oil to an engine of a car. If you want your car to run smoothly, you must regularly get your oil changed. The same goes for a relationship in order to maintain a great relationship you must communicate on a regular basis. Communication can make or break a relationship. The great thing about effective communication is that it can be learned and accomplished. Here are a few key points on how to communicate effectively.

1. Listening

Listening is a very important part of effective communication. When you are a good listener, you encourage your partner to talk openly and honestly. Make sure you allow the other person to speak without interruptions. This reassures your partner they have your full attention and your genuinely interested. 1 Corinthians 13:4, says. "Love is patient." Listening is also a great sign of being patient. Listening will show your partner that you genuinely care for them.

2. Be Confident In Speaking

Learning how to communicate is vital for a relationship's survival. You must learn to open your mouth and talk to one another. If you are not effectively communicating how will your partner know when you are hurting? Or how will they know when you are happy or disappointed? Some issues can be quickly resolved by simply speaking and being honest with one another. Your partner won't know until you talk to them. It's unfair to think they already know what's wrong or automatically know your thoughts. It may be uncomfortable, BUT TALK! It may be hard to express your emotions, BUT TALK!

3. Honesty

Be open and honest with your partner. Some people have never been open with their partner. Hiding your emotions from your partner or pretending everything is alright is never good in a relationship. Nor giving the silent treatment is healthy either. Being open means discussing topics you may have never discussed with another person. Allow yourself to be vulnerable and honest. After allowing yourself to be vulnerable and honest, be prepared for possible hurts and disappointments. Never allow the fear of possible disappointments or hurt, keep you from being open and honest with your partner.

4. Stay Focused

I must remind you that at some point your communication may turn into an argument, but always remember to respect one another. Agree to disagree, but never dishonor or disrespect the other person. While discussing issues, always remember to stay focused on the topic. Don't allow yourself to become distracted or wonder off on different rabbit trails because nothing will get resolved. Staying focused on the topic of discussion is a sure way to dissolve any issues.

5. Build Trust

Good communication builds trust! Exchanging ideas, messages, or information by speech are effective ways to build trust. Without trust a relationship can't function. When communication is not present, trust suffers.

6. Sense of Humor

Every conversation in a relationship should not be serious. There should be some conversations where you can laugh and joke with each other. If you are truly friends, a sense of humor is needed. It's great to have someone laugh at your jokes and just to have fun with. It's also great that you can just be yourself with someone. You don't have to worry about being perfect or walk on eggs shells by saying the wrong thing.

You can have a level of freedom by having fun with the person you love. When you are able to laugh and joke with your partner, this shows that you enjoy each other.

Being able to communicate effectively will help eliminate arguments which can occur regularly in your relationship. Overall, communication should serve these four different purposes:

1. To Inform

Be the first person to tell your partner something before they find out elsewhere. You don't want to make your partner feel like you are withholding information or keeping secrets.

2. To Express Feelings

Your partner can't hear your thoughts. They need to know if something is bothering you. Expressing your feelings will strengthen your relationship.

3. To Gain Understanding

Every relationship has to evolve. You will learn new and different things about each other as time goes. Having effective communication establishes a greater understanding of each other.

4. To Meet Social Expectations

When the communication is effective, you will know each other's boundaries. You will know your partner's beliefs and values. You will know their overall expectations in life and other areas.

APPLICATION QUESTIONS

1. Why is communication important in a relationship?

2. What are the five purposes of communication?

3. What are the six keys points of having effective communication?

4. Why is listening an important part of communication?

CHAPTER 21

PUT A RING ON IT

Is your relationship becoming more serious? When will you know it's time? Here's a few ways to know if it's time to put a ring on it.

1. **You feel like you can trust each other with your deepest secrets. You tell each other all there is to tell about one another, including:**
   - The highs and the lows, the good, the bad, and the ugly.
   - The successes and failures, joys and sorrows.
   - Promotions, demotions, emotions, she-motions, and the he-motions.
   - You both have shared the same stories at least three or four times.
   - You have no more skeletons in the closet.

If you have talked about these things, it's time to put a ring on it.

2. **Your love for them overrides all their flaws.**
   - You can still love them at their worst when they've failed miserably.
   - They've ripped your heart out, and you still love them and still want to be with them.
   - You've seen her without makeup and her fancy hairdo or when she's not dressed up, but you're still attracted to her. Or, you've seen him with a five-o'clock shadow and wearing his favorite holy tee-shirt, but still, you'r attracted to him.

When your love for them is earnest and covers a multitude of sins (1 Peter 4:8), it's time to put a ring on it.

3. **You're comfortable enough around them to pass gas. You can be transparent and let your guard down.**
   - You can talk about poop
   - You let out loud burps
   - You're not afraid to fart in front of one another. You are extremely comfortable around them. Excuse me, but that seals the deal.

When you pass the fart contest or test, it's really time to put a ring on it.

4. **You respect their space and give them their freedom.**
   - You respectfully allow each other to do their own thing.
   - She can hang with the girls on a girl's night out, and you allow him to hang with his guy friends.

When you find the right balance, without controlling one another. It's time to put a ring on it.

5. **You aren't afraid to get messy together.**
    - You aren't worried about being cute and eating proper.
    - You can pig out in front of one another.
    - You can leave sauce on your lips or gravy on your chin, and you can laugh about it.

When you aren't afraid to indulge in greasy, sloppy foods together and have hilarious moments, then it's time to put a ring on it.

6. **You feel like you can't live without one another.**
    - You're lonely without them.
    - You can't imagine your life without him or her.
    - You feel like you both can trust one another.
    - You are inseparable.
    - You can't go to sleep without calling to say goodnight.

If you are on each other's mind constantly, and you miss them every moment you are apart. It time to put a ring on it.

7. **You have eyes only for him or her.**
    - You learn to adjust or mesh or gel with his/her family.
    - You aren't swayed by the attractiveness of others.
    - You don't fanaticize about being with someone else.

When the only person you want is them, then it's time to put a ring on it.

APPLICATION QUESTIONS

1. What are the signs to know when to put a ring on it?

   _____
   _____
   _____
   _____
   _____

2. How do you know if the one you are dating can be trusted?

   _____
   _____
   _____
   _____
   _____

3. Why is it important to be comfortable with each other in a relationship?

   _____
   _____
   _____
   _____
   _____

4. What are some ways to respect each other's space?

_____
_____
_____
_____

ABOUT THE AUTHOR

Dr. Ron Webb is the pastor of the Mt. Calvary Powerhouse Church in Poplar Bluff, Missouri. Pastor Webb has been in the ministry for over 33 years. He attended Three Rivers College in Poplar Bluff, Missouri. He majored in Business Administration and was a former "Raider" basketball player. He earned a Bachelor's of Theology from the International College of Bible Theology, and a Master's of Pastoral Studies and a Doctorate of Theology from Midwest Theological Seminary.

The unique ministry of Dr. Ron Webb is evident as he is anointed in the areas leadership and church government. Dr. Webb has been considered by many to be "A Pastor To Pastors". His ministry is centered around "Restoration" and "Racial Reconciliation" and a sincere belief that we must "Reach the Lost at Any Cost". His preaching and teaching focuses on empowerment and hope. He often says that church is where you go, but ministry is what you do outside the walls of the church. Many outreach ministries have been birthed to address the unmet needs of the church and local community.

Dr. Webb is the C.E.O. and President of the S.E.M.O. Christian Restoration Center, a center for individuals who might need a second chance on life. He is the founder and a lead instructor of "School of the Prophets Bible College" in Poplar Bluff, Missouri. He is also the founder of the Heartland Family Center, an emergency shelter for families, an outreach ministry that was founded in 2007. The Heartland Family Center is owned and operated by the Mt. Calvary Powerhouse Church. Covenant Ministries is another ministry that was designed by Dr. Webb to advance God's Kingdom by providing a fellowship in which men and women of God find mutual encouragement, edification, counsel, and participate in leadership and ministerial training. Dr. Webb serves as the Bishop of Covenant Ministries. He is a sought after speaker, who has ministered the gospel of Christ both national and internationally, including Canada, Haiti, Russia, Jamaica, and England. Dr. Webb is active in the community and has served on both local and state level boards.

Dr. Webb is an accomplished writer who has authored several books on leadership and racial reconciliation, including "Leadership from Behind the Scenes" and its companion workbook. This book focuses on challenges of Leadership, a must read for anyone in a leadership role. "Destroying the Roots of Racism", where he invites us to be a part of the solution, and urges those hurt by racism not to let the adversity destroy their character, but instead let it define their character. "Exposing the Enemy from Behind the Scenes" (a sequel to Leadership from Behind the Scenes) to equip both established and emerging leaders to recognize the spirits that have infiltrated the church and stunted kingdom advancement. His latest book "Leadership Lessons: Things I Wish They'd Told Me" a minister's manual full of information and examples that will help new leaders to navigate challenges and move forward into their ministry. Also he authored, "Exit Plan."

Dr. Webb is married to Georgia Webb and they have 3 children: Ronnie Jr., Tony, and Jackie (Webb) Brown all of Poplar Bluff, Missouri, and three grandchildren: Jerrell Brown, Jr., Jaxson Brown, and Tony Webb, Jr. In his leisure time, Dr. Webb enjoys fishing and playing sports.

You can check out Dr. Webb's Relationship video that went viral by <u>clicking</u> here or going to https://youtu.be/0DkWLZvZ3wQ.

REFERENCES

1. "Fornication." Merriam-Webster.com. Merriam-Webster, n.d. Web. 14 Mar. 2018.
2. "Courtship." Merriam-Webster.com. Merriam-Webster, n.d. Web. 15 Mar. 2018.
3. "Bait." Merriam-Webster.com. Merriam-Webster, n.d. Web. 13 Mar. 2018.
4. Shotgun Theory." Urbandictionary.com. Urban Dictionary, n.d. Web. 16 Mar. 2018
5. "Sanctification." Merriam-Webster.com. Merriam-Webster, n.d. Web. 16 Mar. 2018.
6. "Blended Family." Merriam-Webster.com. Merriam-Webster, n.d. Web. 16 Mar. 2018.

INDEX

A

abandonment, 91
abstinence, 45
abusive relationships, 61, 63–65
afflictions, 17
agenda, 28
application questions, 11, 14, 18, 22, 32, 35, 38, 42, 45, 56, 59, 64, 68, 73, 77

B

baggage, 5, 16, 72, 79–82
balance, 72
believing, 29, 31
blessings, 13, 27, 53, 86, 88
Boaz, 4, 85–87
boundaries, 2, 30, 89, 97
boyfriend, 17, 72
breakup, 5, 20–22, 75–76

C

character, 29, 105
children, 26, 52–54, 58, 70, 73, 105
choices, 8, 44
commitment, 2, 38, 44, 66, 89, 91
communication, 94, 96–98
compromise, 27, 72

control, 27, 41, 61, 76
counterfeits, 52
couples, 6, 29, 66, 71
courtship, 6, 27, 31, 107
credit score, 54
culture pressure, 45
curse, 3, 9, 81

D

darkness, 30–31
date, 1, 3, 10, 16, 27, 48, 52–55, 70
deception, 24
defrauding, 29
depression, 17, 34
desperate, 34, 49
destiny, 9, 28, 44–45, 67, 82
disappointments, 71, 95
discernment, 63
discipled restraint, 45
discouragement, 34
dishonor, 26, 96
distraction, 22
divorce, 47, 54, 70, 79
divorce rate, 6

E

edification, 105
emotional baggage, 79–80, 82
emotions, 17, 20, 79, 95, 99
empowerment, 104
enemy, 30–31, 35, 41, 45, 76, 81–82, 105

expectations, 2, 59, 97

F

failures, 16, 34, 99
feelings, 18, 21, 23, 79, 89–91, 97
fish, 1, 3, 37–38
focus, 11, 21–22, 37, 44, 76
forgive, 22, 80, 82
fornication, 28–29, 66–67, 107
fornicators, 67

G

generation, 24, 29, 49
God, 3, 5–7, 9–11, 17–21, 25–31, 40–41, 44–45, 48–49, 52–54, 63–64, 66–67, 70, 76–77, 80–81, 84–86
guard, 27, 30, 75, 100
guideline, 3, 6, 27–31, 47–50

H

healing, 1, 5, 10, 17, 81
heart, 1, 10, 14, 17, 25, 27, 30–31, 34, 52, 75, 77, 81, 100
heartaches, 26
heartbroken, 21
heaven, 5, 67
Holy Ghost, 25, 29
honesty, 90, 95
Humiliation, 62

I

idols, 28
insecurities, 75
issues, 4, 30, 54, 71, 95–96

J

journey, 59, 63, 65

K

kingdom, 28, 67, 105

L

leadership, 105
learning, 21, 28–29, 95
loneliness, 17, 34–36
loyalty, 90
lust, 40–41, 53, 66

M

marriage, 1, 9, 12, 14, 20, 27–28, 31, 54, 67–72, 86
marriage counseling, 6
marry, 8, 29, 40, 54, 67, 70, 86
mate, 39, 56, 84
ministry, 6, 31, 104–5
money, 14, 55, 66, 72

P

pain, 16, 18, 20–21, 79–80

partner, 14, 55, 61–62, 90–91, 93–97
patient, 95
persecution, 80
pray, 21, 41, 49, 63–64, 76–77, 81
prey, 16, 35, 75, 77–78
private property, 40–43
promises, 26, 89–90
prosperous marriages, 6
protection, 63, 86

R

rebound, 17–18
recovery, 20, 22
rejection, 17, 34
relationship, 2–4, 6, 9–10, 14–21, 24–25, 27, 29–30, 48–49, 52–54, 56, 61, 63, 71–72, 82–83, 89–99
replacement, 77
responsibility, 21, 66
revenge mode, 17
righteousness, 40, 42, 75

S

sacrifice, 35, 45, 84
selfishness, 89
setting goals, 48
shacking, 30, 67
shotgun, 44
Shotgun Theory, 107
singleness, 1, 10
singles, 2–3, 5–6, 47
soaking season, 4, 13–15

sorrows, 53, 99
standards, 32, 47–48, 58, 90
strengthen, 2, 11, 41, 84, 91, 97
support, 72, 89, 91
support system, 55

T

tongues, 75
traumatic event, 79
trials, 37, 55, 90
trust, 10, 25, 31, 55–56, 77, 96, 99, 101

U

unmarried person, 8

V

Verbal Insults, 62
victim role, 21
vision, 48, 58, 89
vulnerability, 16

W

wholeness, 63, 65
wisdom, 30
women, 5, 8, 13–14, 34, 38, 52, 54, 85, 105

www.ingramcontent.com/pod-product-compliance
Lightning Source LLC
Chambersburg PA
CBHW070055120526
44588CB00033B/1557